CAGE AND AVIARY SERIES

BICHENO FINCHES

THEIR CARE

AND BREEDING

OTHER TITLES AVAILABLE OR IN PREPARATION

CAGE AND AVIARY SERIES

Canary Standards in Colour by G T Dodwell
   Special Edition with 32 colour plates of canaries extra, ready for framing and
   de-luxe binding
Canary Breeding for Beginners by James Blake
The Border Canary by Joe Bracegirdle (second edition) (limp)
The Fife Canary by T Kelly and James Blake (limp)
The Gloster Canary by James Blake (limp)
The Norwich Canary by K W Grigg and James Blake (limp)
The Roller Canary Revised by George Preskey (limp)
The Yorkshire Canary by Ernest Howson (hardback)
The Yorkshire Canary by Shackleton (limp) Reprint of Classic
Lovebirds by Ian Harman (limp)

BUDGERIGAR BOOKS

The Budgerigar Book by Ernest Howson (hardback)
Budgerigar Breeding for Beginners by James Blake (limp)
Cult of the Budgerigar by W Watmough Revised by Cyril Rogers (limp)
   There is also a hardback edition with more coloured plates
   This is the standard work on Budgerigars
Inbreeding Budgerigars by Dr. M D S Armour Revised by Cyril Rogers (limp)
World of Budgerigars by Cyril H. Rogers (limp)
   History of the Fancy and the Mutations

OTHER CAGE BIRDS

Cage Bird Hybrids by Charles Houlton Revised by James Blake (hardback)
Gouldian Finches by A J Mobbs (hardback)
World of Zebra Finches by Cyril Rogers

BICHENO FINCHES

THEIR CARE

AND BREEDING

by

A J MOBBS

NIMROD PRESS LTD.,
15 The Maltings,
Turk Street,
Alton, Hants.
GU34 1DL

Printed by: PTARMIGAN PRINTING CO.

NIMROD PRESS LTD.,
15 The Maltings,
Turk Street,
ALTON, Hants.

CONTENTS

ILLUSTRATIONS

BICHENO FINCHES

FOREWORD

The Bicheno is a delightful Australian Finch which, although attired in only black, browns and white, is nevertheless most attractive. Due to Australia, in 1960, placing a ban on all exportation of its fauna, captive stocks (outside Australia) became somewhat low during the 1970's, but as Australian Finches gained in popularity, so the Bicheno slowly gained in numbers.

One of the main problems experienced by potential breeders of this small finch is the difficulty in obtaining true pairs. This is due to the difficulty in sexing by visual means. The author describes an almost infallible method of sexing, which will no doubt prove helpful to those who, in the past, have given up any attempt to breed the Bicheno because of their inability to identify correctly true pairs.

Never before has a book been published which deals solely with the Bicheno Finch and it is hoped that this in-depth study will encourage more aviculturalists to take up the species, thus ensuring its availability to future bird keepers.

For those interested in the Bicheno (and other species of Australian Finch), membership of the Australian Finch Society is recommended. The Society was formed in 1971, its aims to promote all aspects of keeping, breeding and exhibiting Australian Finches. The AFS produce six excellent magazines per year and has branches throughout the UK. Membership is world-wide and further details can be obtained from V. Langley, 478 New Hey Road, Wirral, Merseyside L49 9DB. When writing for information, a stamped, addressed envelope (or for those overseas an international reply coupon) should always be enclosed.

```
***********************************
*                                 *
*                                 *
*               1                 *
*                                 *
*                                 *
*       THE  BICHENO  FINCH       *
*                                 *
*          IN  THE  WILD          *
*                                 *
*                                 *
*                                 *
***********************************
```

Figure 1-1 Bicheno male (white rumped race)

Figure 1-2 Bicheno Female (black rumped race)

CHAPTER 1

BICHENO FINCH IN THE WILD

BRIEF HISTORY

The Bicheno Finch was named by Vigors and Horsfield after J.E. Bicheno, secretary, at the time to the Linnean Society of London, from specimens in the Society's museum. These had been discovered by Brown at Shoalwater Bay and Broad Sound (Queensland), in September 1802.

In Australia the species is usually referred to as the Double-Bar Finch. Other names include Banded Finch (for the white rumped race), Ringed Finch (for the black rumped race) and Owl or Owl-faced Finch. In the UK the name most commonly used is Bicheno Finch.

DISTRIBUTION

Two subspecies of the Bicheno Finch are recognised, *Poephila b. bichenovii* which has a white rump is found in Eastern Australia and *P. b. annulosa* which has a black rump, is found in the Top End and Kimberley Regions. The two interbred in a broad area, south of the Gulf of Carpentaria. It appears the species range has expanded towards the coast in the lower Eastern Queensland and the South-east Regions. It has also expanded southward in the Murray-Darling and South-east where, before 1900, there were no records (see Blakers, M. et al (1984). The Atlas of Australian Birds).

FIELD NOTES

In the wild the Bicheno Finch lives in close-knit groups, containing around 40 birds. It is always near water, usually in woodland with a grassy understorey, but also in acacia scrub and cultivated land such as parks, gardens and such-like.

The Bicheno feeds mainly on the ground on small seeds of grasses and other plants. It is often found in cleared areas,

3

Figure 2-0 Australia: Home in the wild.

4

which confirms the impression that it has benefitted by settlement clearing.

Flight is rather weak, the birds usually flying from bush to bush, avoiding long flight in the open. The species roosts either in small unlined nests, built for the purpose, or in old breeding nests of its own or other species. Often several individuals will roost in one nest.

In Northern areas the Bicheno breeds mostly during the second half of the wet season, sometimes later. In Eastern Australia it breeds mainly in Spring and Autumn but nests can be found almost throughout the year.

DESCRIPTION: *P. b. bichenovii*

Adult Male

The adult male Bicheno is about the size of a Zebra Finch, but with a longer and somewhat graduated tail, shorter tail coverts and a smaller beak. Although it possesses no bright colours, its shapeliness and its somewhat delicate and pleasing patterned plumage gives it a beauty equal to many of the often more gaudy Australian Finches.

The forehead is black; crown dull brown to reddish brown with faint darker cross-barring shading to light greyish brown to silver grey, with more pronounced fine darker cross-barring on the hind neck, mantle, back and lesser wing coverts. Most of the wing is black, delicately spotted with white on all parts of the feathers that show when the wing is folded, except for the ends of the outer primaries. Under wing coverts are creamy buff. The rump is white and the long feathers from the centre of the rump reach down over the black of the upper tail coverts so that the latter appears white. Tail is brownish black. Face, including area above the eyes and ear coverts, silvery white, encircled by a narrow black band running from forehead, around the cheeks and across to divide the throat from the breast. The breast itself is silvery white, sharply divided by

5

another narrow black band across the lower breast. Remainder of underparts are creamy white. Under tail coverts are black. Bill is greyish blue, darkest on top of the culmen. Irides are dark brown; legs and feet greyish blue to dark grey.

Adult Female

The female averages a little smaller than the male and may have a more greyish white face. Also the breast is often more of a greyish white rather than the silvery white of the male. Many state that the breast bands are narrower in the female, but I have been unable to discern any significant difference (see page 39 for a more easy method of sexing).

Juvenile

Immature birds are more brown above with less pronounced markings; those of the wings being buffish or dull white and barred rather than spotted. Breast bands are usually present; however, some immature birds lack either one or both breast bands with the whole of the underparts being greyish white, darker on the breast which may vary from grey to pale grey. The beak is blackish as are the legs and feet.

p.b. annulosa

Adults as for *p.b. bichenovii*, but with the rump entirely black. It is reported in the literature that immature of this race lack the black breast bands. I have not found this to be so (see page 46 for further details).

GENERAL BEHAVIOUR

Call-notes

Lost calling is a plaintive 'twoo-twoo' (Immelmann, K. (1982) in Australian Finches in Bush and Aviary, describes this call as sounding like 'tiaat, tiaat'). Social calling is similar to that of the Zebra Finch and is a repeated 'tat, tat'. The lost call (or locating call) is loud for such a small bird. Social calling (or contact call) is much more subdued.

Song

There appear to be two types of song; the advertising song being fairly loud, the courtship song more subdued. The former can usually be heard when a male finds itself alone, although young birds which have just moulted into adult plumage may use the song even when in the company of others of either sex.

When singing, the bird will remain stationary and take up an alert upright position, with head held high. The song is continuous and may be uttered for lengthy periods if the bird is not disturbed. However, when another Bicheno (of either sex, but especially a female) appears close-by, the singing bird becomes silent.

As already mentioned, the courtship song is more subdued and is best described as a soft oft repeated buzzing note. Indeed, so soft is the song, one has to be no more than 2m away from the bird to hear it. Often the courtship display is enacted in complete silence and, from my observations, the courtship song is used only rarely.

Courtship and Display

During the actual display, the body plumage of the male is fully fluffed so that the body appears spheroid. The bird crouches over the perch, parallel to the female with his head turned towards her. In this position he may sing and/or bill-wipe. Morris, D. (1958) in the Comparative Ethology of Grass-finches (Erythurae) and Mannikins (Amadinea), 'Proceedings of the Zoological Society of London', 131: 389-439, mentions excessive bill-wiping in his description of the courtship. This is not something I have witnessed; indeed, many of the males I have observed have failed to bill-wipe at all during the courtship ceremony.

Should the female move away, the male will chase after her

7

and again take up the postures described above. A responsive female will, in a matter of seconds, after courtship has begun, crouch down on the perch and with quivering tail, invite the male to mount her. Copulation takes place immediately.

Compared with many species of Australian Finch, the courtship display of the Bicheno is fairly simple and is often quickly over. Indeed, many males, when presented with a female in full breeding condition, rarely take up courting postures at all, but chase after her for a few seconds, after which copulation takes place without further preliminaries.

As far as I am aware the use of a nesting symbol in the display of the Bicheno Finch had not before been described until my notes appeared in the 'Avicultural Magazine', Vol. 91, 3, pages 166-167 (1985). The dried grass used is usually some 200mm in length and is unlike that which would be used for nest-building, being somewhat thick and not in the least pliable.

I have never witnessed males taking up the grass, but have always encountered them when the grass was already being held in the beak. Throughout the sequence, the male faces his respective female; he then gives a series of bows with the beak held in a horizontal position at all times. As the male becomes upright after each bow, the legs are stretched to their utmost and the feet (on occasions) appear to leave the perch (no more than 3 mm). The sequence may be carried out for two or three minutes, after which the grass is released. As I have only witnessed the sequence when it was already underway, it is not possible to estimate the full length of time it may be carried out.

Social Behaviour
The Bicheno is highly social and usually of a peaceful nature. However, fighting will occur between adult males when in breeding condition if housed together with females in the close confines of a cage. Allo-preening and clumping occurs habitually between flock members as well as between male and

female of a pair. As the species is highly social, much stress can
be caused if a single specimen is housed on its own.

Figure 1-3 Fully feathered at 6 weeks of age

```
*********************************
*                               *
*                               *
*               2               *
*                               *
*         PURCHASING            *
*                               *
*           STOCK               *
*                               *
*                               *
*                               *
*                               *
*********************************
```

Figure 2-1 Cage for transporting birds

CHAPTER 2

PURCHASING STOCK

The ideal way in which to purchase good breeding stock is to contact a successful breeder. The name and addresses of such people can be found in a current membership list of the Australian Finch Society (see Foreword); alternatively, breeding stock can be found in the sales columns of the weekly journal "Cage and Aviary Birds", or a similar publication.

CHOOSING THE BIRDS

Due to the minute size of young Bicheno Finches, many breeders are reluctant to close-ring any youngsters they breed. If potential stock is close-ringed, then the year of birth is obvious. For those birds which are not, the date of birth should be ascertained at the time of purchase; the birds can then be fitted with coloured and numbered split rings so that accurate records can be maintained.

Bichenos attain full adult plumage at approximately 8-10 weeks of age. The moult from immature to adult plumage is not as critical as in the Gouldian Finch (when losses often occur); nevertheless, it is preferable to purchase only those birds in adult plumage as, to move stock at any age causes a certain amount of stress and immature birds could succumb if moved at such an early age.

It is possible to have Bichenos sent by rail, but to collect potential stock from a breeder in person is always preferable as one is then able to observe how the birds are housed and fed. A show cage or similar should be taken along when intending to purchase stock. To place a newly purchased bird or birds in any box which comes to hand is certainly not the ideal way to transport them, especially if a long journey is to be undertaken.

Food should be supplied, the ideal being a piece of spray millet taped to the rear of the cage, next to a perch. Even for a long journey there is little need to supply drinking water. However, water should be offered the moment one arrives home with the birds.

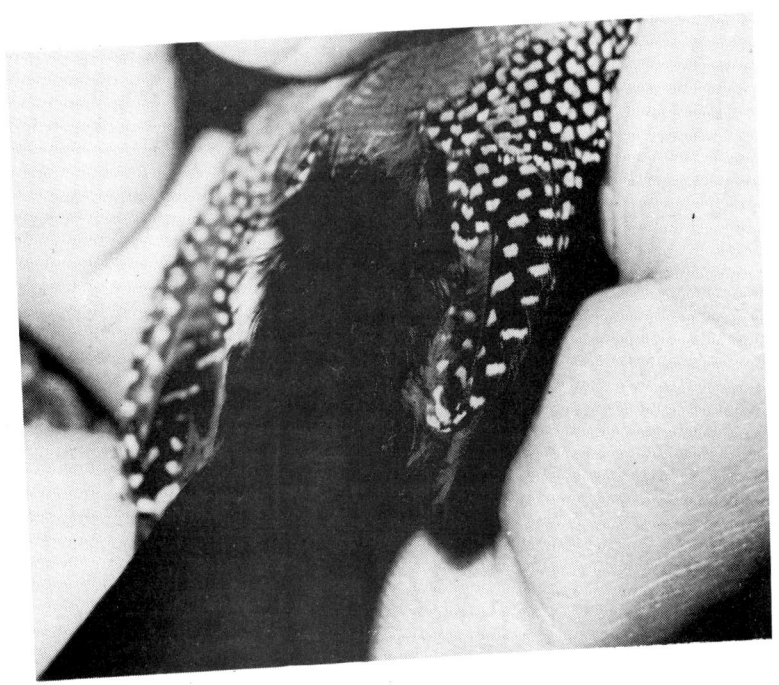

Figure 2-2 Bicheno Black Rumped Race

3

ACCOMMODATION

Figure 3-1 A typical Small Aviary for Bicheno Finches

CHAPTER 3

ACCOMMODATION

Bicheno Finches can be housed in aviaries, indoor flights or roomy cages. Some of the advantages and disadvantages of each system are outlined below.

AVIARIES

Although I have never housed Bichenos in aviary accommodation, many do so with seemingly good results. A breeding pair would no doubt fare well in a communal aviary as long as the other occupants were of a similar size. However, I certainly would not recommend that Bichenos and Zebra Finches be housed together as the latter could prove too much of a nuisance by interfering with the nests of the former. Also, Bichenos will hybridise with the Zebra Finch and there is a possibility of this taking place. Such hybrids would only be a curiosity and would be worthless and a waste of good breeding stock.

I am not keen on aviaries containing mixed species and feel that, should a birdkeeper prefer to house his or her birds in an aviary, then one given over to a single species is preferable. The aviary would need to be well-planted with small shrubs and/or bushes, thus enabling the birds to seek out their own nesting sites. Plenty of soft hay, coconut fibre and suchlike would have to be supplied, preferably tied loosely into small bundles and attached to a perch or shrub for easy access.

Care should be taken not to disturb the birds once they have commenced nesting operations, especially when chicks are near to fledging. Young birds leaving the nest prematurely could easily be lost, especially during a sudden rain storm.

Figure 3-2 Typical cages for breeding

18

Shelter

A well-lit shelter would be a necessity and it would be preferable if all feeding utensils were placed inside the shelter. Bichenos cannot be classed as a hardy species by any means and because of this should be housed in an aviary from late May until early September, after which they would have to be transferred to a warm birdroom.

Suitability

There is little doubt that Bichenos can be bred successfully in aviary accommodation, especially in countries which enjoy warm, dry summers. In the UK, and much of the Continent, such summers are often few and far between and, because of this, I feel indoor accommodation is preferable for these more temperate climates.

INDOOR FLIGHTS

Flights indoors could be utilised for Bicheno Finches and would no doubt prove suitable for colony breeding if the enclosure were of a reasonable size. However, such a flight would take up as much room as a block of cages and, as there is more control over caged birds, I can see no advantage in keeping the species in indoor flights.

A reasonably large flight would no doubt prove suitable for moulting and growing on young stock (or for resting adults), but the former would have to be watched carefully when first released into the flight (especially if they had been cage-bred), to ensure they found the food and water containers easily.

Bichenos are rather weak flyers and flight (as well as aviary) accommodation would need to be furnished with an abundance of thin, natural perches to enable the birds to move around freely.

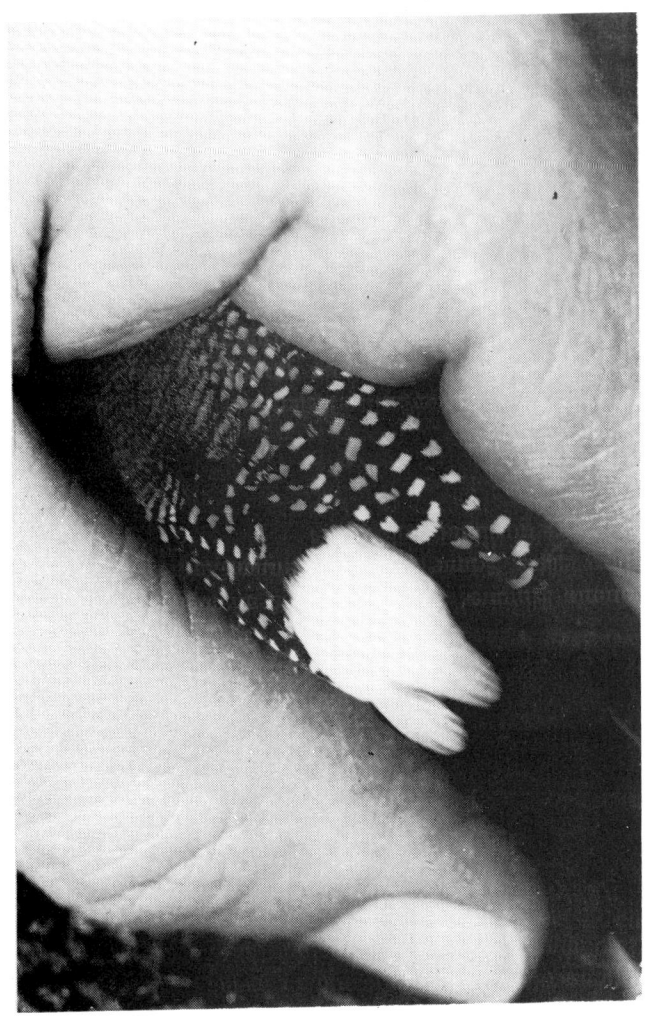

Figure 3-3 Bicheno White Rumped Race

BICHENO FINCHES

CAGES

With modern day gardens becoming increasingly smaller, many birdkeepers find it difficult to give over valuable space to aviaries and many house their birds in roomy cages either in an outside birdroom or in a room in their dwelling house.

The majority of Australian Finches take readily to cage life; Bichenos being no exception. A box-type cage, 91cm x 41cm is ideal for this species. Such cages can be made in blocks with an overall length of 1.8m. Made this way, a divider can be placed in the centre. This can then be removed after the breeding season and the 1.8m cage will prove ideal for young birds and/or resting adults (no more than ten birds per cage).

Painting

All my cages are painted pale green on the insides, black on the outsides including the cage fronts. If a good quality vinyl emulsion is used, it is not only easily wiped over with a damp cloth, but it does not build up in layers as does normal gloss paint. Therefore, there is never any need to strip the paint off before applying a fresh coat each year.

Floor Covering

For a flor covering, I use clean newspaper. Sand can be utilised, but may prove somewhat expensive and difficult to remove during cleaning operations.

MAINTAINING THE BIRDROOM

LIGHTING

Bichenos require fifteen hours of light each day, especially during the breeding season. Daylight type fluorescent tubes are ideal as they provide a shadowless light which reaches all parts of the room and does not throw what could be alarming shadows into the birds' cages.

Figure 3-4 Bengalese Hen (Dilute Chocolate and White). All colours are suitable as fosters.

are switched on at 6 a.m. and turned off at approximately 9 p.m.

Nightlights

A small 11 watt nightlight bulb is left burning during the night period. If only Bichenos are housed in the birdroom, then possibly the nightlight could be dispensed with; it does, however, help combat the problem of night fright (although Bicheno Finches are not particularly prone to this). If one's birds are housed in an outside birdroom, then a nightlight is a necessity, especially if one is plagued with roaming cats.

TEMPERATURE

Bichenos, when breeding, require a temperature of around 18°C. During the non-breeding season, this could be lowered to approximately 15°C.

HEATING

The ideal way to heat a birdroom is with a good quality electric fan heater, used in conjunction with a reliable thermostat. To save on heating costs it is advisable to insulate outside birdrooms and to double-glaze windows of both outdoor and indoor accommodation. Tubular heaters which consume electricity at low cost may be used as background heat.

BATHING FACILITIES

Bicheno Finches are keen bathers and should be supplied with bathing facilities at least every other day. For birds housed in aviaries or large indoor flights, a fairly large, shallow dish (no more than 4 cm in depth) should be kept in the enclosure at all times. It would require cleaning and replenishing each day. For caged birds, a bath should be made available every other

Figure 3.5(a) Adequate electrical facilities essential. Example shows
sockets, switches and automatic controller for lights

Figure 3-5 (b) A typical heater suitable for cage birds.
(Tubular heaters are an alternative)

day. I have found the ideal receptacle to be a 12 cm plastic flower pot saucer. These can be placed in the cages first thing in the morning, to one side of the cage, well away from the food containers and perches. The bathing receptacles should be removed at lunchtime, thoroughly washed and dried and stacked in the birdroom ready again for use.

When a number of birds are housed in a 1.8m flight cage, the area where the bath is placed can become extremely damp and this can be damaging to a cage made of wood. To avoid this, self-adhesive vinyl may be laid on the area where the bathing saucer is placed, thus preventing continual dampness on the wood of the cage.

Many birdkeepers use plastic hang-on type baths as manufactured for pet birds. These can be hung permanently on the cage front, over the open door. However, I am wary of such baths when young Bichenos first leave the nest as it is possible they could enter the bath and not find their way out before becoming saturated in water. In such a condition they could soon become chilled and eventually die if not found in time.

```
* * * * * * * * * * * * * * * * * * * * * * * * * * * * * *
*                                                         *
*                                                         *
*                                                         *
*                          4                              *
*                                                         *
*                       D I E T                           *
*                                                         *
*                                                         *
*                                                         *
*                                                         *
*                                                         *
* * * * * * * * * * * * * * * * * * * * * * * * * * * * * *
```

Figure 4-1 From left to right: Plain canary seed, white millet, Japanese millet, spray millet

CHAPTER 4

DIET

BASIC FOODS

The basic diet for Bicheno Finches should consist of good quality white millet, plain canary seed and Japanese or panicum millet - I see no reason to supply both, especially if spray millet is available at all times. Many birdkeepers offer a mixture (referred to as Foreign Finch Mixture) which contains all these seeds (although this mixture usually contains panicum rather than Japanese millet), and supply it in either an earthenware bowl on the floor or in a hopper attached to the wall of the cage or enclosure. I prefer to supply seeds in separate dishes as I find Bichenos take more Japanese millet (or panicum) than anything else and to supply a mixture can cause a considerable amount of waste, due to the birds throwing out the seeds in an attempt to find the small millets.

Bichenos will rear healthy youngsters successfully on a diet of seed alone, but it is certainly beneficial to offer other foods. I supply fresh, thoroughly washed lettuce three times a day to birds with chicks and to young birds until they have completed their first moult, but only once every other day to resting adults and incubating pairs. It is important to offer only the green leaves from the lettuce; the very pale green or whitish leaves from the centre are never eaten. The birds just pick them over and then ignore them.

SOAKED SEEDS

Soaked seeds consisting of 50/50 budgerigar mixture are offered all the year round; breeding birds (with young) should be given as much as they will consume, as should young birds. Non-breeding and incubating adults are given one dish each day. Soaked seeds are taken avidly if the seeds have just begun to sprout. Well sprouted seeds arc usually ignored and those showing no signs of sprouting are only picked over.

To ensure a continual supply of soaked seeds, I use the following method. Enough seed for one day's feeding is placed into a clean plastic sieve. The sieve is placed inside a 500-gram margarine carton and luke warm water is added until it reaches the top of the container. The container is then placed in a 12cm plastic flowerpot saucer (in case of water spillage) and placed on a shelf in the birdroom. The seed is left to soak for a two-day period during which time the water is emptied away, the seed is rinsed under a running tap and fresh water is added at least twice during the 48 hour period. When the soaking is completed, the seed should be given a final rinse under a running tap, left to drain for about a quarter of an hour, then tipped into a 12cm plastic flowerpot saucer, which is covered with another saucer of the same size. The seed is then left in the warm birdroom for 24 hours, when it should be ready for use. Two sieves are used, one always being one day in advance of the other. Thus, to have a continual supply of soaked seeds, one requires two sieves, two margarine containers and four 12cm saucers.

During the warmer months of the year, the seeds will usually sprout easily over a three-day period. However, during the colder periods, a little heat may have to be supplied if the seed is to sprout sufficiently. Moreover, if all the seed from one soaking is not used at once, it must be covered, otherwise it will quickly dry out and much of its attraction will be lost to the birds.

I find 250 grams of seed is enough for a breeding stud comprising eight to ten pairs, and their progeny. For larger studs, more soaked seeds would, of course, be required. However, the procedure would be exactly the same. Using the above method, rarely if ever is one troubled with mould appearing on the soaking seeds. Should mould appear, it must be removed immediately; the easiest way is to remove it with a spoon.

OTHER FOODS

Spray Millet

Bicheno Finches are extremely fond of spray millet and this should be made available at all times. To save cluttering up the cage front with too many clips, I have devised a method of attaching the spray millet to the back wall of the cage (see fig. 4-5).

Minerals

Bichenos take large amounts of cuttlefish bone and, as well as that supplied in a clip attached to the cage front, all my birds receive flaked cuttlefish bone at least twice a week. Laying hens are given small amounts of flaked almost every other day until the clutch has been completed. Mineralised, oyster-shell and limestone grit is always available. These items are placed together in a small dish on the floor of the cage. Every week, whether or not the contents have been eaten, the dish should be emptied, washed thoroughly and replenished. Some Bichenos will take charcoal granules and a teaspoonful is placed on the floor of the cage, next to the grit dish, about once a week.

Another source of minerals which is avidly taken is Kilpatrick's Iodised Minerals. This can usually be purchased either loose or in small polythene bags from most shops dealing in pigeon requisites. These minerals resemble charcoal granules, but are of a finer texture. They are offered in the same way as the charcoal, placing a teaspoonful each week next to the dish containing grit. Both charcoal granules and the minerals are eaten almost immediately, so there is little possibility of either becoming fouled with droppings.

Some Bichenos will take shells from hens' eggs. These are first placed in water which is allowed to simmer for approximately two or three minutes, after which they are taken out and left to dry. They can then be stored in a screw-top jar, ready for use. I do not crush the egg shell, but crumble it slightly in my hand before placing a few pieces on top of the grit. Not all Bichenos will take these shells, and any which is uneaten after 24 hours is always removed from the cage and discarded, otherwise it may become fouled with droppings. Bichenos of all ages may sample the egg shell and it should be offered about every four or five days.

Live Food

It is reported in the literature that Bicheno Finches take live food in the form of insects, especially when they have young in the nest. No doubt birds housed in outside aviaries would obtain many insects amongst the shrubs and bushes. However, it may prove difficult to provide insects to caged birds (I have never attempted to do so). Bichenos appear to be not in the least interested in mealworms.

Soft Food

Many Bicheno pairs with young will take a good proprietary brand of egg food, especially when their chicks are from one to 14 days of age. Some pairs will give this food to their chicks for the whole of the rearing period. Such food requires mixing fresh each morning and any left after 24 hours must be discarded. I have never provided egg food in a separate dish, but always placed small amounts in the same dish with the soaked seeds.

DRINKING WATER

Fresh water for drinking must be available at all times. For caged birds it is best supplied in a clipper fount attached to the cage front. Aviary birds would no doubt drink from the baths; nevertheless, it is preferable to give a separate supply for drinking purposes either in clipper founts or in small jam jar founts.

Figure 4-2 Soaking Seeds
Left Hand: Soaked seed just after being placed in saucers
Right Hand: Soaked seed already sprouted and ready for use

Figure 4-3 Mixed Seeds (see text) being soaked

33

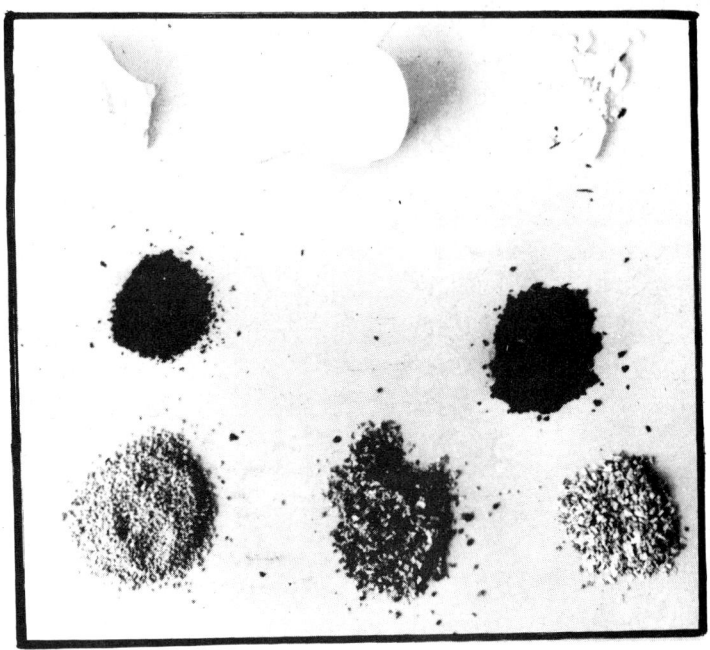

Figure 4-4 Essential Minerals.
Left to Right:
Top row: Cuttlefish Bone, Hen Egg Shell, Flaked Cuttlefish Bone.
Centre: Kilpatricks Iodised Minerals, Charcoal Granules.
Bottom row: Grits—Limestone, Mineralised, Oyster Shell.

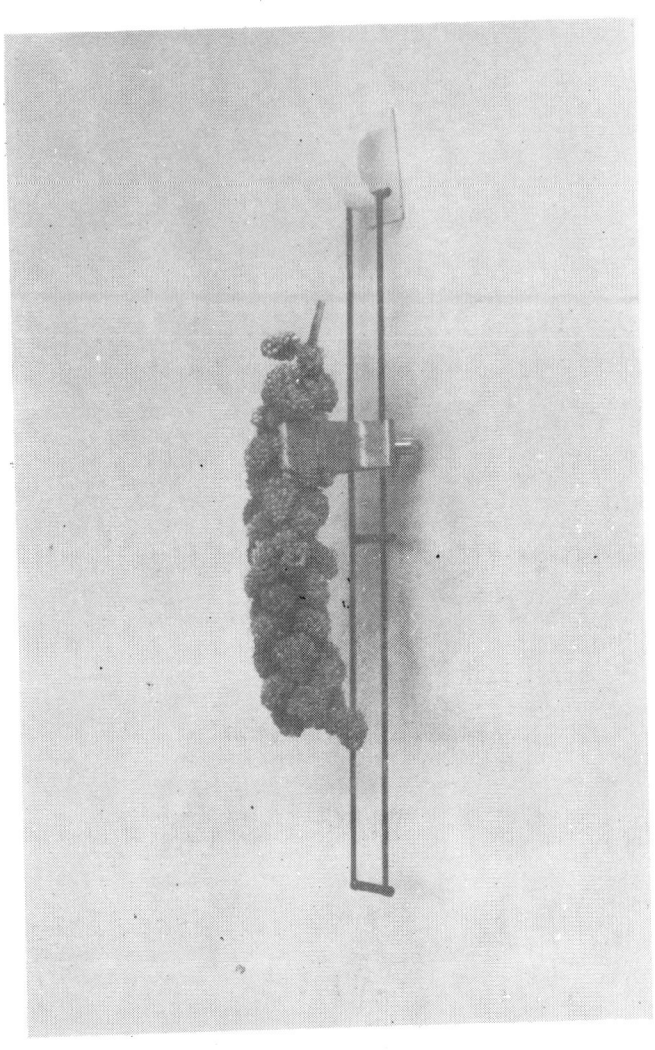

Figure 4-5 Spray millet holder. Designed and used by the author. It is attached to the back wall of the cage, thus helping to keep seed husks in the cage rather than on the birdroom floor.

```
* * * * * * * * * * * * * * * * * * * * * * * * * * * * * * *
*                                                             *
*                                                             *
*                                                             *
*                           5                                 *
*                                                             *
*                      B R E E D I N G                        *
*                                                             *
*                                                             *
*                                                             *
*                                                             *
*                                                             *
* * * * * * * * * * * * * * * * * * * * * * * * * * * * * * *
```

Figure 5-1 Nest box used for Bicheno Finches

CHAPTER 5

BREEDING

If housed and cared for correctly, Bicheno Finches can prove extremely prolific, a good breeding pair producing chicks readily.

SEXING

Probably the main reason more Bichenos are not bred each year is the difficulty many have in sexing these birds correctly. Two males housed together in a breeding cage never sing, and as they will be seen to enter the nest-box regularly (and roost in it), although no eggs are forthcoming, their owner will often leave them together for some time in the hope that they are a true pair.

Two females housed together eventually begin to lay eggs and, upon inspecting the nest-box, one may find anything up to 12 eggs. One can then be certain that both birds are female.

Many birdkeepers attempt to sex Bichenos by visual means. Males supposedly have brighter face masks and chests than females. This may prove correct in certain cases, but what does one do when confronted with an exceptionally well-marked female or a poorly marked male?

To use the following method, which I have found to be most reliable, at least two birds are required and preferably they should have been housed together for at least a fortnight or more. If one considers they are not a true pair, remove one of the birds to a cage on its own. If either bird is a male, then within seconds of being placed on its own, it will commence to sing. It is noticeable that a male will, the moment it is caged on its own, stand in an alert position on the perch, hardly moving at all. It may call for a moment or so, but will then begin to sing.

If the bird is female, it will prove extremely restless, moving from perch to perch continually and, although it may call, it obviously will not sing. As mentioned, a male caged on its own will sing almost immediately; however, to ensure that a non-singing bird is, in fact, a female, it is prudent to leave the bird caged on its own for at least two or three minutes as, although I have yet to encounter a male which did not sing within seconds of being placed on its own, to be completely sure a non-singing bird is female, one should at least give it the opportunity to prove otherwise.

So accurate have I found this method of sexing, I can sex a cage of up to ten birds within half an hour. It is preferable if the birds about to be sexed are in full adult plumage, although young males which are not often attempt to sing when placed on their own.

All my young stock is housed in cages which can be divided down the centre and it is a simple matter to segregate the birds when I wish to sex them. It should be mentioned that the divider must be solid (mine are of plywood), as the bird on its own must be unable to see others of its kind.

BREEDING TIMES

Bichenos can be used for breeding from approximately nine months of age. If used before this age, it may result in the loss of females due to egg binding.

It is possible to have different pairs breeding throughout the year, but I much prefer a fixed season as each year cages may require renovating and they will certainly need a thorough cleaning and a coat of paint annually. This chore could prove difficult to carry out if birds were breeding all the year round. I suggest, therefore, that all breeding pairs be placed in their respective cages at about the same time.

Second year (or older) females housed in resting cages will, soon after the annual moult is completed, begin to lay eggs on the floor of the cage. First year birds will, at approximately nine months of age, also begin to lay. Because of this, if one follows my suggestion regarding a fixed breeding season, it is preferable to retain for breeding young birds from the second nest of the season rather than from the first, as those from the second nest should be ready for the breeding pen as soon as the older birds have rested and completed their annual moult.

NEST-BOXES

Although Bichenos are the smallest of the Australian Finches, they do appear to prefer a fairly roomy nest-box; a 13cm cube being ideal. The front opening of the box should be no more than 4cm wide; this means that the front panel needs to be 8cm in height. A hinged lid should be fitted, thus allowing easy inspection of the nest and access to the chicks. This is most important if one intends to close-ring the chicks.

The nest-box should be hung in a rear corner of the breeding cage, allowing approximately 10cm between the top of the box and the roof of the cage. The opening should face the centre of the cage. It is important to allow a 10cm space between the top of the nest-box and the cage roof as many male birds spend much of their time sitting on top of the box while the female is incubating.

NEST BUILDING

Under caged conditions Bichenos rarely attempt any form of nest building, preferring to accept a ready-made nest in the box provided. Because of this, before placing the nest-box into position, I always add a layer of clean white sawdust or shavings and then fill the box with a mixture of soft hay and coconut fibre. A small amount of nesting material is placed on the floor of the cage (under the nest-box so that it does not become soiled with droppings), but rarely do the birds use this extra

41

material. However, males will often take up pieces of hay as nesting symbols (see page 8).

A breeding pair will usually enter the nest-box almost immediately they are released into the breeding cage. Even those which are a little shy of the box will enter for the night period and from then on use it regularly. Occasionally a pair of first-year birds may prove so shy of the nest-box they will not enter, even for the night period, preferring to roost on the top of the box. After three or four days, if the birds refrain from entering the box, place an 'L' shaped piece of wood on the top of the nest-box (see figure 5-2) which will deny access to the top of the box. Rather than sleep on a perch, the birds will enter the nest-box for the night period and, after a few days, the wood can be removed.

INCUBATION

As Bicheno chicks usually hatch within a day or so of each other, I presume the species does not commence to incubate in earnest until the second or third egg is laid. It is often difficult to establish the actual day incubation begins as one, or both, of the breeding pair may remain on the nest for lengthy periods during the day and, of course, the pair will always roost in the box, even without eggs. However, if one or both birds remain on the nest when food dishes are being replenished, then one can be almost certain incubation has commenced.

The average clutch is four and chicks begin to hatch after 12 days. At first they are minute and it is difficult to discern how many chicks there are if one takes only a perfunctory glance.

Nest Inspection

To obtain the maximum breeding potential from a pair, regular inspection of the nest-box is essential, otherwise a pair could be left to incubate infertile eggs. Inspection will also prevent the loss of chicks if the parent birds are not feeding them correctly as they can be removed and placed under fosters.

An incubating bird should never be forced off the nest. If the birds are never found away from the nest, then a light tap on the side of the box will usually persuade them to vacate. Once the nest has been inspected, the box should be replaced into position and one should then leave the birdroom immediately so as to allow the birds to settle back on the nest. To remain in the birdroom may inhibit the birds as many Bichenos are loath to re-enter the nest while their owner is in the birdroom.

Nest inspection need not be carried out daily; indeed, with this species it could prove detrimental to do so. When the birds have been incubating for about seven days, an inspection should be carried out. Infertile eggs can be recognised at a glance as they appear paler in colour than fertile eggs. Once the breeder becomes used to the appearance of infertile eggs, there is little need to remove the whole of the clutch for inspection. If the whole of the clutch proves infertile, remove it, place fresh material in the corner of the cage and, in a matter of days, the birds should begin to nest again.

If only one or two eggs are fertile, these can be removed and either given to another pair of Bichenos or fostered under Bengalese. However, if a Bicheno pair are allowed to hatch and, hopefully, rear the chicks from only two eggs, it is preferable to leave the whole of the clutch with the birds, since removal of all but two of the clutch may prompt the birds to desert.

It is a waste of breeding potential to allow a Bicheno pair to rear a single chick; therefore, if only one egg hatches from a clutch, the chick is best fostered out to another pair of Bichenos or Bengalese with a chick or chicks of a similar age.

REARING THE CHICKS

Unlike many species of Australian Finch such as the Gouldian,

Figure 5-2 Bicheno nest containing 5 eggs

Bichenos do not appear to have a set pattern when breeding. Because of this, I can only describe the average breeding cycle taken from details kept on a number of pairs.

As already mentioned, newly hatched Bicheno chicks are minute. They are flesh-coloured and covered with white down. The down is almost lost and the flesh darkens within 3 to 6 days. At about seven days of age, the primaries begin to appear. At this age the parent birds appear during the day to brood only spasmodically and, by the ninth day, brooding ceases altogether, although both parents will sleep in the nest-box at night.

Both parents feed the chicks, often entering the nest-box at the same time. When the chicks are ten days old, if they have been well fed, it is possible to close-ring them. One should not attempt to do so before this age and it is often possible to close-ring chicks of up to 13-14 days of age.

Chicks begin to leave the nest at approximately 28 days. At around this age they can prove somewhat delicate and any which appear unable to return to the nest-box should be gently caught up and placed in the box. Otherwise they may become chilled and can then quickly succumb and die. Even those chicks which have not left the nest-box prematurely will at first spend only short periods out of the box. As they become more mature, so they will spend longer periods away from the nest, but will always return to roost.

Chicks can be removed from the parent birds at approximately 6 weeks of age; left longer, the parent birds (especially the female) are liable to attack them.

SECOND NEST

The moment the chicks are removed from the breeding cage, the cage should be thoroughly cleaned, the nest-box emptied of its contents, washed, refilled with nesting material and placed back in position. It is imperative this is carried out immediately the chicks are removed as the female will almost certainly commence to lay a further clutch within a matter of days. Indeed, many will begin to lay before the chicks of the first clutch are old enough to be removed. Should this be the case, then the nest-box should be removed, the eggs carefully placed in a container and the box emptied, thoroughly cleaned, refilled with nesting material and, after gently replacing the eggs, returned to the cage.

To persuade a female to take to a cleaned nest is remarkably easy if, for nesting material, coconut fibre only is used as this is easily formed into a nest hole. Often the chicks will refuse to enter the freshly cleaned box, but prefer to roost on the top. This is an advantage for, if they return to the box to roost, then in all probability the eggs will become soiled, and may even be chipped or broken.

Although Bichenos can prove most prolific, as with all domesticated birds, it is advisable to only allow each pair to rear two rounds each season. This means that when the second round of chicks have been reared, the female will often lay a further clutch, even after being placed in the resting cage. Such eggs should be collected up the moment they are found and either discarded or, if one is not against the use of fosters, placed under Bengalese, as these eggs almost invariably prove fertile.

GROWTH OF CHICKS

When first they leave the nest, Bichenos are only half the size of an adult. Many will have pin feathers on and around the head, and the tail feathers at the most will only be half grown.

Chicks which have been well fed have the same feather pattern as an adult except that the colours are much more subdued, a point discussed in Chapter 1. Chicks which have not received a sufficiently nutritious diet often have only the top black breast bar, others may have no breast bars at all. Chicks marked thus always moult out normally, attaining the usual adult plumage with the first moult.

Bichenos begin their first moult at approximately 6 weeks of age and well fed youngsters attain full adult plumage within 8-10 weeks. Because the species attains full adult plumage at a relatively early age, many breeders are tempted to use young birds for breeding far too early. Many hens can be lost because of this, due mainly to egg-binding. Although young Bichenos appear fully adult at approximately ten weeks of age, if such birds are compared with adult birds (of 7 months or more), it will be noticed that the younger birds are usually smaller. Bichenos will continue to mature until they are at least 6-7 months of age. Therefore, one should never use a bird for' breeding until it is at least 9 months of age.

Many young hens will begin to lay eggs at this age. If they do, it is a good sign they are ready for breeding.

CLOSE-RINGING

As already mentioned, Bicheno chicks can be fitted with a close-ring at anything from 10 to 14 days of age (certainly no later). At this age the parent birds will have ceased to brood the chicks during the day so there will be little need to wait for the former to vacate the nest-box before removing it. However, as Bichenos always roost on the nest at night and, as pairs may go to roost fairly early in the evening, it is best to close-ring the chicks first thing in a morning. An ideal time being when the fresh supply of soaked seeds has been placed in the cage, as the parent birds will be keen to investigate the seeds and this will keep them occupied while the breeder is close-ringing the chicks.

The chick should be taken up in the hand and placed in the crook of the fingers with the head resting on one's index finger. The leg and rear toe should be held between thumb and forefinger with the front toes pointing straight ahead. To keep the toes together, draw them through the fingers which have been moistened liberally with saliva, straightening the toes at the same time. The ring is then slipped over the toes, eased over the joint and finally over the back toe.

Split Rings

Being so small, many breeders are reluctant to close-ring Bicheno chicks as they feel they may damage them. If this is the case, then the chicks should be fitted (at the time of weaning) with a split celluloid ring. These can be obtained in virtually any colour or colour combination and may also be numbered consecutively if one wishes. A tool is always supplied with these rings and they are easily fitted.

Although I close-ring all the birds I breed, I often use split rings on adult birds as a means of identifying each individual without first having to catch up the bird to ascertain details on its close-ring.

FOSTERING

From my experience, the majority of Bicheno Finches make excellent parents and, once one has established a strain of good breeding birds, there is little need for fosters. Should, for some reason, a pair refuse to rear, their chicks could be fostered out either to other Bichenos or to Bengalese.

A Bengalese may appear to be somewhat large to use for fostering; however, they are quite capable of rearing Bichenos and are certainly preferable to Zebra Finches, mainly because the latter are so much like Bichenos in many ways; there could be problems with imprinting.

I have, on occasions, fostered out deserted chicks to other Bichenos who have chicks of a similar age, especially if the latter has only one or two chicks of their own. I have never experienced problems when doing this, the 'foster' pair taking immediately to their new chicks.

If one decides to keep a few pairs of Bengalese for fostering, they can be offered the same diet as the Bicheno Finches except that charcoal granules and Kilpatricks Iodised Minerals need not be offered.

It is sometimes mentioned that Bengalese used for fostering should be housed in cages far smaller than those recommended for Australian Finches. The reason given is the need for the foster chicks to be close to the Bengalese at all times if they are to be fed correctly. All my Bengalese cages are approximately the same size as those used for Bichenos and rarely have I experienced problems with Bengalese not feeding their foster chicks. Should a pair prove to be poor feeders, then they are discarded as to even allow them to rear young of their own may result in the chicks carrying on the trait.

I have noticed that Bicheno chicks up to approximately five weeks of age always return to the nest-box to be fed (by their natural or foster parents); because of this, the cage size is irrelevant.

It is sometimes recommended that once fostered chicks have left the nest, the box should be removed. Some even go as far as to recommend that any chicks remaining in the nest-box after one or two have fledged should be removed from the box and placed on the floor of the cage. I am totally against such a practice. Bicheno (and many other Australian Finch) chicks can soon become chilled at this early age and require the warmth of the nest-box at such a critical stage of their development. Also, Bengalese are always so attached to their nest-box it would no doubt cause stress if it were removed.

Invariably, Bengalese will produce a further clutch of eggs by the time their foster chicks are ready to be weaned. But so accommodating are these birds that, once the Bicheno chicks have been removed, the nest-box can be thoroughly cleaned, refilled with fresh nesting material, the eggs replaced and the Bengalese will then continue to incubate regardless of the disruption.

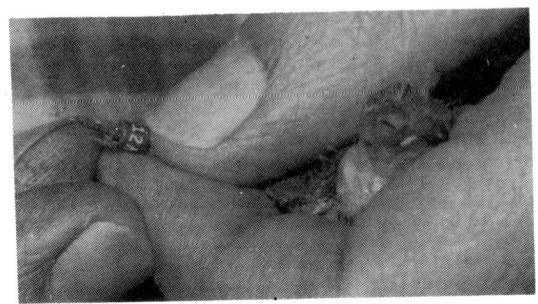

Figure 5-3 Fitting (a) a closed ring
(b) a split ring to a Bicheno chick

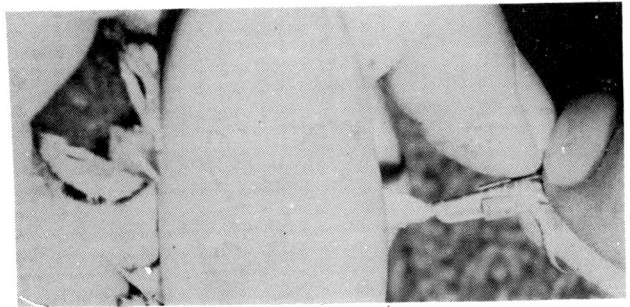

```
*  *  *  *  *  *  *  *  *  *  *  *  *  *  *  *  *  *  *  *  *  *  *  *  *  *  *
*                                                                            *
*                                                                            *
*                                                                            *
*                               6                                            *
*                                                                            *
*                       RUMP   COLOUR                                        *
*                                                                            *
*                       INHERITANCE                                          *
*                                                                            *
*                                                                            *
*                                                                            *
*  *  *  *  *  *  *  *  *  *  *  *  *  *  *  *  *  *  *  *  *  *  *  *  *  *  *
```

6

RUMP COLOUR

INHERITANCE

Figure 6-1 Bicheno chicks 4 days of age

Figure 6-2 Bicheno nest containing 5 eggs

CHAPTER 6

MATING EXPECTATIONS

At the time of writing (1987), no mutations have appeared in the Bicheno Finch. There are two subspecies; one with a white rump, the other has a black rump.

In the past, certain authors have mentioned the delicacy of the white rumped race, others have found the black rumped to be so. From my experience, both subspecies appear equally robust.

From records kept on a number of breeding pairs, I have compiled the following mating list as a guide to the rump colour inheritance in the Bicheno Finch.

MATINGS LIST

Rump Colour	Abbreviations Used
White rumped	WR
Black rumped	BR
White rumped split for black rumped	WR/br

Adult Pairs	Percentage of Progeny
a) WR x WR	100% WR
b) BR x BR	100% BR
c) WR x BR	100% WR/br
d) BR x WR/br	50% BR; 50% WR/br
e) WR/br x WR/br	25% WR; 50% WR/br; 25% BR

It must be emphasised that the above list is only offered as a *guide*; also the percentages used in (d) and (e) are statistically derived and will be found to be true only when dealing with large numbers. Further investigation into the mode of inheritance in the rump colour of the Bicheno needs to be carried out before it can be fully understood. As so few black rumped birds are available to aviculture at present, it may be some time before any definite conclusions can be reached.

Mating (a) is self explanatory and the percentage quoted is correct as long as the adult birds are *pure* WR's. The black rumped race is recessive and therefore mating (b) is certain to produce 100% BR's. The percentage quoted for mating (c) would also be as stated, but only if the WR were *pure*. With mating (d), should the WR/br have a number of black feathers (or black marked feathers) on the rump, it is possible more than 50% of BR birds would be produced. Normally mating (e) would only be used as a last resort, as with most mutations, it would prove impossible to identify the normals (WR) from the splits (WR/br). However, as the Bicheno does not appear to follow the usual pattern of inheritance, it is possible to identify split birds (WR/br) by the black feathers (or markings) on the otherwise white rump. It is possible that some white rumped birds from this mating could also be split for black rumped, but as there would almost certainly be a percentage of youngsters with black feathers or markings on the rump, it would be preferable to class these only as splits and all white rumped as pure. Should one or both of the adult pair have black markings or feathers on an otherwise white rump, then the percentage of WR/br's and BR's would almost certainly be greater than those quoted in the matings list.

MELANISM

Melanism can occur in the Bicheno and is most probably caused by incorrect feeding or lack of sunlight during the moult. A male bird I owned was, at the time of purchase, almost completely black on the breast and also had black instead of dull brown on the crown, hind neck, mantle, back and lesser wing coverts. After using the bird for breeding, it was moved to a resting cage with other males. After its moult, its plumage reverted to normal.

Figure 6-3 Bicheno chicks 10 days old

Figure 6·4 Bicheno female - Black rumped race

```
* * * * * * * * * * * * * * * * * * * * * * * * * * * * * * * *
*                                                             *
*                                                             *
*                                                             *
*                                                             *
*                            7                                *
*                                                             *
*                       H Y B R I D S                         *
*                                                             *
*                                                             *
*                                                             *
* * * * * * * * * * * * * * * * * * * * * * * * * * * * * * * *
```

ALBINO

Cock: beak coral red, eyes clear red, feet and legs pink, all feathers pure white without any markings of any kind.
Hen: same as cock but with a little paler beak.

Figure 7-1 A Hybrid Bicheno X Zebra Finch
(Foreign Birdkeeping, A.G. Butler)

CHAPTER 7

HYBRIDS

From the literature it appears the Bicheno Finch has hybrid-ised with a number of species of Australian Finch and also with the domesticated Bengalese. In Cayley (1932), "Australian Finches in Bush and Aviary", there are two colour plates depicting hybrid finches. Plate X (opposite page 222), depicts among others, three crosses between the Bicheno, namely Yellow-rumped x Bicheno, Long-tailed x Bicheno and Bicheno x Zebra. There are details of the Bicheno x Zebra hybrid (pages 67-68) and the Yellow-rumped x Bicheno (pages 95-96). There are also details of Cherry Finch x Bicheno hybrids (pages 221-222).

The Bicheno x Zebra appears to be the most commonly produced hybrid. The cross has occurred in both directions. It is not clear if any of the hybrids were fertile. Some authors have reported that all are sterile; others mention fertile males.

Nowadays, any attempt to breed hybrids from Australian Finches would be frowned upon and it is doubtful if any serious breeder would purposely place two birds of a different species together in the hope of producing hybrids.

Anyone producing a hybrid, either deliberately or by accid-ent, should keep notes on the breeding and submit a detailed report and full description (with a drawing or photograph if possible) to a recognised avicultural journal.

Many of the crosses (listed below) seem almost unbelievable (i.e. Bicheno x Bengalese), and unless written reports are submitted for publication, many would find the resulting progeny from such crosses difficult to visualise.

BICHENO FINCHES

LIST OF REPORTED HYBRIDS

MALE		*FEMALE*
Bicheno Finch	x	Zebra Finch
Bicheno Finch	x	Long-tailed Finch
Bicheno Finch	x	Parson or Black-throated Finch
Bicheno Finch	x	Masked Grassfinch
Bicheno Finch	x	Cherry Finch
Bicheno Finch	x	White-headed munia
Bicheno Finch	x	Bengalese Finch
Parson Finch	x	Bicheno Finch
Long-tailed Finch	x	Bicheno Finch
Cherry Finch	x	Bicheno Finch
Zebra Finch	x	Bicheno Finch
Yellow-rumped Finch	x	Bicheno Finch

The only hybrid I have actually seen alive is the Zebra Finch x Bicheno Finch.

```
* * * * * * * * * * * * * * * * * * * * * * * * * * * * * * *
*                                                           *
*                                                           *
*                                                           *
*                                                           *
*                                                           *
*                          8                                *
*                                                           *
*                   E X H I B I T I N G                     *
*                                                           *
*                                                           *
*                                                           *
*                                                           *
* * * * * * * * * * * * * * * * * * * * * * * * * * * * * * *
```

Figure 8-1 Zebra Finch Society Show Cage

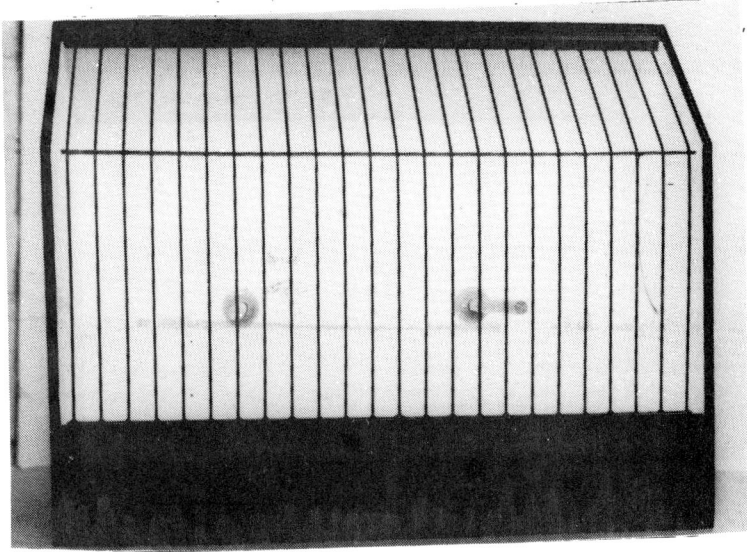

Figure 8-2 Recommended Cage (see text)

CHAPTER 8

EXHIBITING

Bicheno Finches can be exhibited singly or in true pairs. As a good pair will invariably be placed above a good single, it is preferable to exhibit true pairs if possible.

THE CAGE

The species is often exhibited in a Zebra Finch show cage. However, I would recommend a cage 45cm long, 25cm wide by 30cm high as the ideal; anything smaller does not show the birds to advantage. Natural perches, rather than dowelling, not only enhance the overall appearance of the show cage, but would, if placed in suitable positions, also show the birds to advantage. Bichenos are continually on the move and perches of natural wood (approximately 1cm thick) should be placed in such a position as to allow the birds to move around the cage in a natural manner.

STANDARDS

There is no standard for the Bicheno Finch; nevertheless, pairs should be as well matched as possible. Both birds should have clear cut markings, especially around the face and on the breast. The black and white wing markings should be well defined. Birds with missing claws, overgrown, chipped or crossed beaks should not be used for exhibition.

Although there are few black rumped specimens available at the present time, perhaps it should be mentioned that when Bichenos are shown in pairs, the two sub-species should not be mixed.

BICHENO FINCHES

CAGE REQUIREMENTS

Bichenos will spend a considerable amount of their time on the floor of the stock cages and during quiet periods between judging, they may spend some time on the floor of the show cage. Because of this, it would be prudent to cover the show cage floor with clean absorbent paper, rather than seeds. Seed and water for drinking would, of course, have to be supplied and would be best placed in the containers usually supplied with show cages as, to place food and water in loose pots on the floor of the show cage, could cause problems when the cage was being moved by the stewards.

Cage decoration is not required and, if used, would not only detract from the overall appearance of the exhibit, but could cause damage to the bird's plumage.

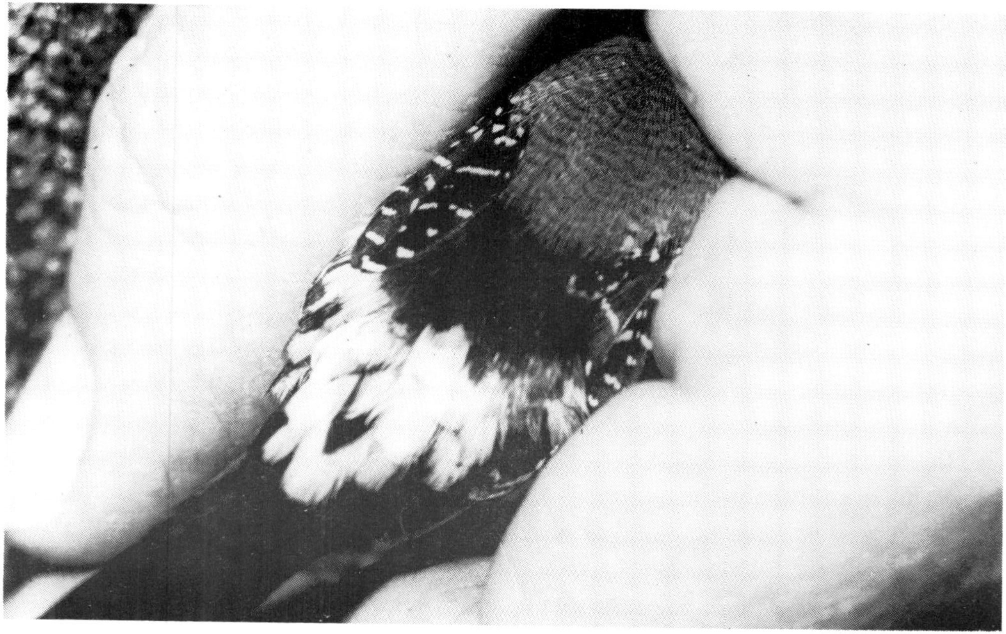

Figure 8-3 Bicheno split black rumped

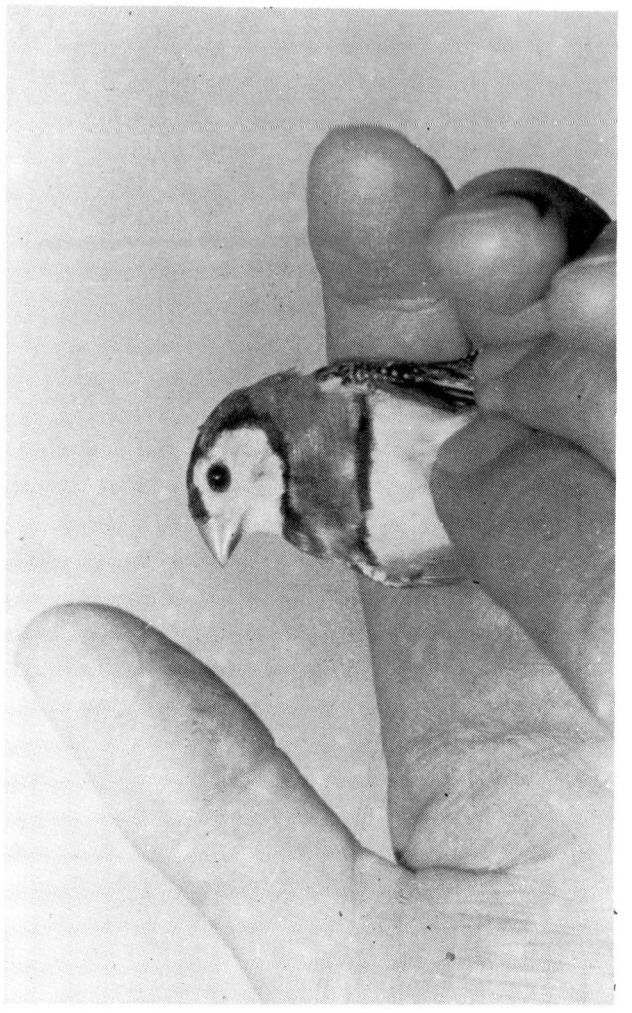

Figure 8-4 Melanistic Bicheno male (note blackish breast)

```
*  *  *  *  *  *  *  *  *  *  *  *  *  *  *  *  *  *  *  *  *  *  *  *  *  *  *  *
*                                                                            *
*                                                                            *
*                                                                            *
*                                                                            *
*                                                                            *
*                      APPENDIX                                              *
*                                                                            *
*                                                                            *
*                                                                            *
*                                                                            *
*                                                                            *
*                                                                            *
*  *  *  *  *  *  *  *  *  *  *  *  *  *  *  *  *  *  *  *  *  *  *  *  *  *  *  *
```

APPENDIX

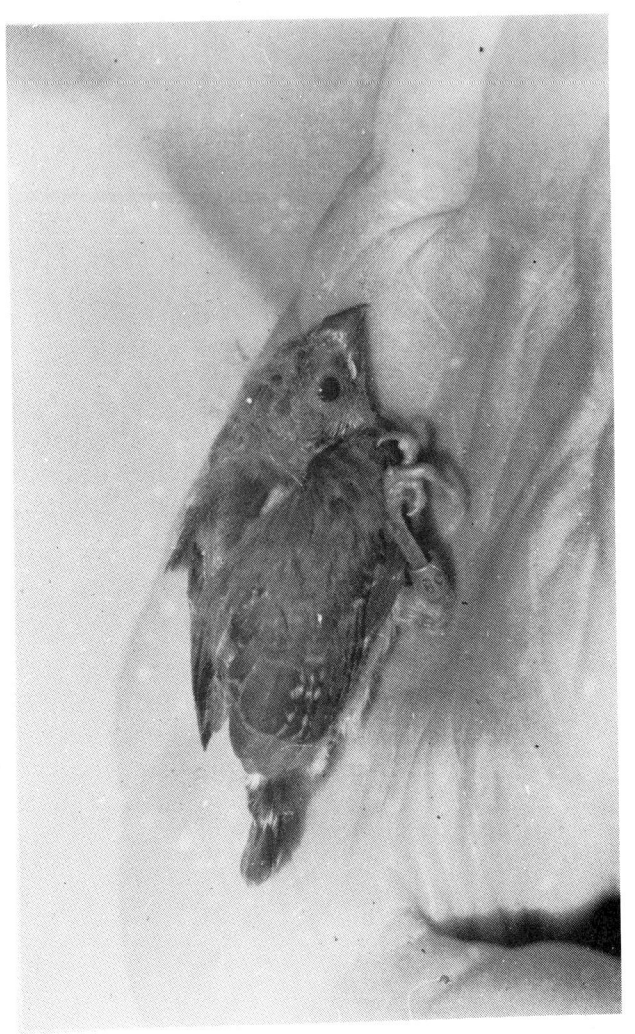

Figure A1 Bicheno chick 16 days old

APPENDIX

FURTHER READING

Rather than a Bibliography, many titles of which would give only brief details and/or descriptions of the Bicheno Finch, I offer a list of titles in which fairly substantial references are made. Obviously not only on the Bicheno, but other Australian Finches also.

JOURNALS

Over the years, many notes and articles on the Bicheno Finch have appeared in the *"Avicultural Magazine"*, journal of the Avicultural Society. One can also find articles in issues of *"Foreign Birds"*, journal of the Foreign Bird League. More recently, much can be found in the *"Grassfinch"*, journal of the Australian Finch Society.

BOOKS

Some of the titles mentioned below are long out-of-print and, being scarce and much sought after, many may prove difficult to find and, if found, somewhat expensive to purchase. The more up-to-date titles may be borrowed from the local lending library or, if not in stock, most will obtain books from other libraries. Alternatively, 'in print' titles can be purchased from a good bookseller, especially one dealing in ornithological/avicultural titles.

1. M. Blakers, S.J.J.F. Davies & P.N. Reilly, *"The Atlas of Australian Birds"*, Melbourne University Press, 1984. Gives most up-to-date details on distribution.

2. A.G. Butler, *"Foreign Finches in Captivity"*, Brumby & Clarke Ltd. Second edition 1899. The first edition is very rare and can cost anything up to £1,000. The 2nd edition is also fairly scarce and the asking price for a copy would be around the £150 mark. The colour plates are by Frohawk and are excellent.
   If one wishes to read the successes (and disappointments) of yesteryear, this title can prove most entertaining.

3. A.G. Butler, *"Foreign Bird Keeping"*, published by The Feathered World. Part 1. ND, but c 1892. Part I (of a two part set) includes the Grassfinches. Although not so attractive as No. 2 (in this list), there is more information to be found and copies are reasonably easy to find and not too expensive. The author gives details of the care and (in many cases) the breeding of finches and supplies details of the hybrids. There is a black and white line drawing (page 49) of a Bicheno x Zebra Finch hybrid.

4. N.W. Cayley, *"Australian Finches in Bush and Aviary"*, Angus & Robertson, 1932. Long out of print and very scarce. Nevertheless is worth searching for (expect to pay £35-40) as there is much detail on the Bicheno Finch, also hybrids. Colour plates are excellent.

5. D. Goodwin, *"Estrilid Finches of the World"*, British Museum (Natural History)/Oxford University Press, 1982. An excellent book which should be in the library of all who are interested in the Estrilidae. The text is superb, being detailed yet easily understood. The author not only gives details of birds in the wild, but in aviculture also. My only criticism is of the colour plates. Many of the species are entirely the wrong shape, some remarkably so.

6. J. Gould, *"Handbook to the Birds of Australia"*, unabridged

edition. Lansdowne Press, 1972. The first edition of this monumental work was published in two volumes in 1865. The unabridged edition is now out of print, but may be found in the catalogues of dealers in secondhand books. Well worth reading for the details on the early discoveries of Australian birds.

7. A.P. Gray, *"Bird Hybrids (a check-list and bibliography)"*, Commonwealth Agricultural Bureaux (Bucks, England) 1958. An extensive list of bird hybrids with reference as to who bred them. There is also an extensive bibliography.

8. K. Immelmann, *"Australian Finches in Bush and Aviary"*, Angus & Robertson, revised edition, 1982. Due to the many reprints of this title, the colour plates are inferior to the originals (those of hybrids especially so), which appeared in Cayley, 1932 (No. 4).

Although this is the most recent edition, the information on the care and breeding of captive birds is somewhat out of date. However, there is excellent information on birds studied in the field and the book is a 'must' for all who are not only interested in the Bicheno Finch, but all Australian Finches.

9. D. Morris, *"Patterns of Reproductive Behaviour"*, Jonathan Cape, 1970. This is a collection of papers, a number of which are on birds. The paper of most interest to the breeder of Australian Finches is *'The comparative ethology of grassfinches and mannikins'* (pages 399-453. The same title can often be found in paperback (both editions are long out of print).

10. P.M. Soderberg, *"Foreign Birds for Cage and Aviary"*, Book III Finches. Cassell, 1956. Part of a four volume set.

BICHENO FINCHES

There are most attractive lithograph plates (although the Bicheno is only depicted in a black and white line drawing). Much detail on care and breeding which, unfortunately, is now much out of date.

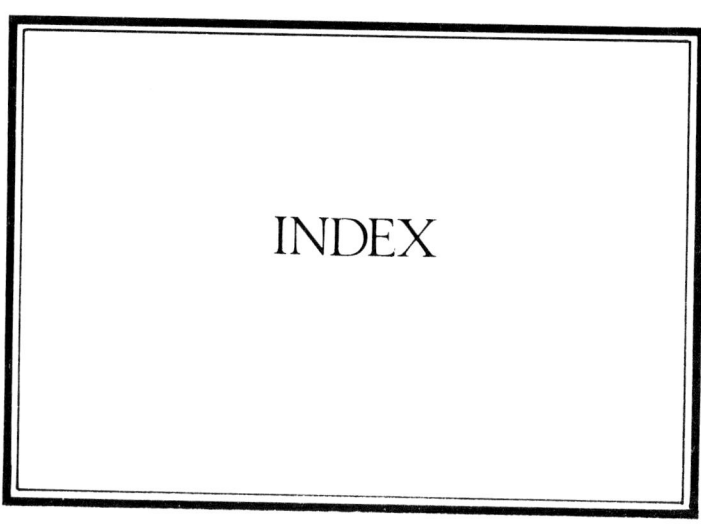

INDEX

INDEX